29 Reasons You Don't Make the Sale and a Solution for All of Them

Category: Business & Economics
Copyright: © 2018
Language: English
License: Standard Copyright License
Author Bob Oros
ISBN: 978-1-387-07208-8

Description: Are you disillusioned by how difficult it is to make a sale? The rewarding life of a successful salesperson is one that is well worth the effort. The financial rewards, the recognition, the freedom, all paint a great picture of what the benefits are. The problem is, it's not as easy as it looks. The buying resistance, the discouragement, the cruel rejection, and the ongoing fight to stay positive, take a toll. It is stressful to leave a secure job and enter a new career in sales. When you announce to your friends and family your plans, you have not yet experienced the pain of defeat and the agony of rejection. It would be too embarrassing to turn back and admit failure. What if you had a roadmap that would cut years off your learning curve? A map that would show you the speedbumps, detours, and roadblocks to avoid. How much would this map be worth to you? Here it is. The map that will help you avoid the 29 reasons you don't make the sale and a solution for all of them.

Key words: mistakes in sales, mental toughness, building confidence, professional selling skills, sell with confidence, confidence in sales, attitude and sales, sales closing techniques, sales training course, sales management training, sales training tools.

ISBN 978-1-387-07208-8

90000

9 781387 072088

Start here:

Are you a new salesperson who is disillusioned by how difficult it is to make a sale?

The highly rewarding life of a successful salesperson is one that is well worth the effort. The financial rewards, the recognition, the freedom, all paint a great picture of what the benefits are.

The problem is, it's not as easy as it looks. Thy buying resistance, the discouragement, the cruel rejection, and the ongoing fight to stay positive, take a toll.

It is incredibly stressful to leave a secure job and enter a new career in sales. When you announce to your friends and family your plans, you have not yet experienced the pain of defeat and the agony of rejection. It would be too embarrassing to turn back and admit failure.

What if you had a roadmap that would cut years off your learning curve? A map that would show you the speedbumps, detours, and roadblocks to avoid. How much would this map be worth to you?

Here it is. The map that will help you avoid the 29 reasons you don't make the sale and a solution for all of them.

This book will be your guide to the success you deserve.

Contents

1. You are not aggressive

Overcoming difficulties means moving towards what you want with the attitude of a winner and taking for granted that you will get it. If you don't have a clearly defined objective and are not consistently moving towards your goals with a positive, aggressive attitude read what it means to be aggressive:

Being aggressive doesn't mean being pushy, it means being mentally strong!

To be successful you have to have a sense of toughness. The more urgent your desire to have mental toughness, the more likely you will be able to endure the hardships and earn the rewards.

Even a slightly less than aggressive attitude will have you back peddling. Never assume you are in the right frame of mind to do battle. You must always reload emotional bullets in your mind.

The aggressiveness begins and takes place in the mind. Aggression is a state of mind that will dominate your thinking process during the adversity that is inevitable. It is about being methodical with a strategy to overcome

5

the threat of quitting. Mental toughness is about your thinking patterns. If you don't have a clear mind, you will have difficulty forming your plan of attack.

Boxers come out of their dressing rooms ready to fight. They are relaxed yet intense with their focus. Although they appear calm, they each have one goal in mind – to win. The best fighters are patient, calculating, and waiting for their opponent to make a mistake.

If a fighter goes down, it's going to take as much aggressive effort to get back up. Only through aggressive determination can you make a comeback. In both scenarios, having an aggressive attitude is essential to either delivering a vicious uppercut or get you back on your feet when your opponent knocks you down. It's all about having the ability to be aggressive at the right time.

2. You are a scavenger

To grow your sales and profits takes a determined, aggressive attitude. Selling in today's environment or ANY environment is not for the person who is only half decided that they are going to be the best.

Don't wait until it's too late and your customers are under attack from your competitors.

General Douglas McCarthy, US Army, knew the cause of failure in two words: "The history of failure in war can be summed up in two words: too late. Too late in comprehending the deadly purpose of a potential enemy; too late in realizing the mortal danger; too late in preparedness; too late in uniting all possible forces for resistance; too late in training our troops."

NOW is the time to make sure you are ready for battle. NOW is the time to be motivated and hungry. NOW is the time to aggressively go after new business.

There are two kinds of animals in the jungle just as there are two kinds of salespeople on the street! HUNTERS and SCAVENGERS. HUNTERS keep their skills

SHARP. SCAVENGERS live on the sales left over from their competitors!

I hope your area or district doesn't come under attack from someone who is a HUNTER, a person who goes after what they want.

General George Patton, US Army, knew the attitude of a HUNTER when he said: "It is the cold glitter in the attacker's eye not the point of the questing bayonet that breaks the line."

Do you have the "cold glitter" in your eye? Are you determined to have the best year ever for yourself and your family? Have you taken the oath to "Do or Die" in your sales territory? Have you taken the oath to not only maintain but to advance, to capture new accounts and to grow your sales?

You might be complaining that it is hard or difficult when customers are not buying. Here's what Admiral Ernest J King, US Navy, had to say about that: "DIFFICULTIES is the name given to things which it is our business to overcome."

You might be complaining that you have been given an impossible task.

Here's what Field Marshal Arthur Wellesley, British Army, has to say: "He who in war fails to do what he undertakes, may always plead the accidents which invariably attend military affairs: but he who declares a thing to be impossible, which is subsequently accomplished, registers his own incapacity."

If I were your competitor I would go after your small to middle size customers that you are taking for granted. The customers who pay their bills on time. The customers that you don't tell how much you appreciate. The accounts that you THINK you have sowed up. I would give them the attention and appreciation you never gave them. I would send them the cards, gifts, and samples that you never thought were important. I would know everything about them.

"In war, nothing is achieved except by calculation. Everything that is not soundly planned in its details yields no result." Napoleon Bonaparte, French Emperor

Why not take the advice of these powerful military minds to plan and execute your sales strategy? Why not aggressively go after more sales, more profits and new customers?

3. You don't establish trust

The reason customers are not interested is because you haven't earned their respect and trust by being an expert in your business.

Trying to skip the most essential ingredient in opening a new account is a huge mistake many salespeople make.

Also, when you are put under pressure to make a sale, this step is not considered important - so it is skipped, and the deal is lost nearly 100% of the time. The way things are out there today this essential ingredient is so essential you wouldn't last a month as a new salesperson unless you realize how important it is.

You are under the gun for more sales. You call on a prospect, dump your sales pitch in their lap and wonder why they don't jump on board with you. You even cut the price so low you are not making any money. They still don't bite. And you wonder how people can be so set in their ways that they won't buy from you. You start looking for someone to blame. You think that your company doesn't offer the right products, or the service is not good enough. Your prices are too high!

Well, all you have to do to see the problem is look in the mirror. And then ask yourself "why should anyone buy from me?" "I'm honest" you might say. "I work for a good company" you might be thinking. "I know my products inside and out" you might be saying, trying to justify your lack of sales. All those things are important, but they don't matter all that much. Just about everyone in sales has the same things going for them. Let's look at it from the prospect's point of view. "I don't care how low your prices are. I don't care how many benefits you have. I don't care if you have the most perfect offer in the universe. I don't know you - so I don't trust you. Period!" So, Job 1 is to establish trust.

You MUST establish trust and respect if you want to make the sale. And today people don't trust or respect anybody unless they have earned it and neither should you. Here is the one way guaranteed to build trust. And if you are a buyer, don't buy unless you established trust with the person doing the selling. In today's economy, everybody is under the gun. They feel the pressure. The heat is on, and some people don't know how to deal with it.

The only way to build trust today is consistent exposure. Consistent exposure means that you make the first call and pick up some information. It means on the second call you pick up a little more information. It means on the third call you bring them an idea that will help their business. On the fourth call you bring them a sample. On the fifth call, you bring them some helpful news, etc. I know what you are thinking I need business NOW.

"I just lost one of my biggest accounts. My income is going to take a huge cut." Well, you should have thought of that 21 weeks ago. That is how many exposures it takes today before someone will really trust you enough to give you their business. Let me say that again. TWENTY-ONE exposures! Are you so confident that you don't need to call on any new business? Are you so sure about your current customers that you know they will never leave you, never go out of business, never switch ownership or a dozen other reasons that can cause you to lose a customer? Are you thinking that because your title is Territory Manager, Marketing Associate, District Sales Manager, Account Manager, Area Manager, General Manager, etc. that your job description is not SELLING? Are you embarrassed to be called a salesperson? If you are, you are missing the whole point of being in business. Those titles are not designed to exclude you from selling; they are there to make the customer view you as something other than someone who is merely trying to sell them something.

But from your point of view, you need to say to yourself "I am a salesperson and proud of it!" What does this mean in sales activities? It means you need to add 10 more prospects to your list and start a "consistent exposure" program with each of them. It means you better not take your current customers for granted. It means you had better be a little more demanding of yourself. You are not pulling your share of the effort it is going to take to pull your company out of the negative situation it is in. It means you are a drag on the system. Trust. You need to be establishing it at a deeper level than ever. It is not who has the cheapest price! It's who do I trust the most with my business?

There are a lot of scammers out there.

Every night on the news you hear about another way someone was taken advantage of, lost their money, lost their house, lost their business, etc. More and more reasons not to trust anyone. And in walks you! You want me to dump my current vendor, and you want me to buy from you! How do I know you are who you say you are? How do I know you have my interest at heart? How do I

14

know you will deliver what you say you will? Those things have to be earned.

After I see you consistently 21 times and you have followed up on some of the things I have asked you about. After you bring me references and testimonials from people I know - and I check you out, then we can talk. Then we will have established a relationship based on mutual trust. Then we can do some business. Try to high pressure me into giving you an order before you have earned it and you might as well never come back. You might as well go work for the government. Because trying to sell in today's business climate without first earning trust is like having the most powerful computer in the world and not knowing that you have to plug it in to make it work! The 21 exposures come from the National Advertising Association. That's how many exposures it takes before someone will trust you enough to buy!

4. You are not a specialist

Years ago there was an essay written about the different types of government. The title of the essay was "The Fox Knew Many Things, But the Hedgehog Knew One Big Thing."

I never read the essay, but the title has an excellent message for us in sales.

We all have some fox in us and know a lot of things, but to be successful in today's competitive market and really build your level of confidence you have to know ONE BIG THING.

It's easy to get sidetracked and become like the fox, who knows all types of things, but here's the problem with knowing all sorts of things, you will not be KNOWN for anything. To have total confidence with your customers, your ONE BIG THING has to be crystal clear in their mind as well as yours. You have to be looked upon as an expert.

If I am buying insurance, I want to buy from a confident person who's ONE BIG THING is insurance. I want to deal with someone who "wrote the book" on insurance.

17

If I am buying or selling a house I want to deal with a confident person who's ONE BIG THING is real estate, NOT someone who is a dental assistant "thinking of getting into real estate on the side!"

Once you decide that selling is the ONE BIG THING you will be happier, healthier and more content with yourself. You will have a higher level of confidence, and your self-esteem will be as solid as a rock.

What keeps you from making the "do-or-die" decision that will give you that solid feeling that you are in control? There are a lot of ups and downs in selling, and when you have a down day, you are at your weakest point. That is when you start to wonder why you have taken on such a stressful occupation. On the other hand, when you have a good day, you wouldn't trade it for anything.

If you look closely at a sailboat tacking into the wind, it seems like it's going back and forth without getting anywhere. If you look at it from a distance, it's easy to see it is heading in a specific direction.

Selling is the same thing. If you look too closely at every presentation, every phone call, every turn-down, it will seem like you are getting nowhere. If you look at the week, month and quarter, you will see that you are making progress toward your goal.

To have the total respect of your customers, you have to be committed to be a professional. You have to be a fanatic about your ONE BIG THING. If you spent just 30 minutes a day studying your products and your profession you would eventually be in the top 10% of your industry.

If I am buying a car, I want the salesperson's ONE BIG THING to be knowledge of the vehicle. If I ask how wide the car's wheelbase is I want them to know without him or her having to look it up.

If I own a restaurant, I want to buy from someone whose ONE BIG THING is selling food and who has a passion for the restaurant business. Someone who can identify with me and "knows where I am coming from."

The biggest reason most salespeople fail is that they never decide that SELLING is their one big thing. They never make the do-or-die decision that THIS IS IT. Once you make that decision and stop thinking about what else you could be doing, your sales will take off.

5. You sell on price not service

How would you like to KNOW with absolute certainty that you could sell anybody? What if you had a magic key that would open the door to everyone you called on? You can! And once you know the secret formula - and apply it - your sales will take off!

You will lose all feelings of call reluctance. Your confidence will double - or even triple. Your income will increase. You will have everything you ever wanted in life.

Here it is...

Find out by careful listening and questioning what your customer wants and let them know that you are sincerely interested in helping them get it.

Too simple? Let's try it on YOU. What do you want most in life? Do you want more cash? A new home? Money in the bank? Financial security?

Now, what if someone came into your life who was sincerely interested in helping you get those things? What if they went out of their way to show you how to increase your income? What if they helped you find ways to save and invest more of the money you work so hard to make so you could become financially secure? What if they helped you find and buy the home of your dreams? Would you want to know this person a little better?

On the other hand what if another person came into your life and all they wanted to do was sell you what THEY thought you should have? If they were overly aggressive, pushy, wanted to get you to do things you were not really interested in - how would you react? Do you see the difference? Wouldn't it feel good to have someone who is sincerely interested in helping you succeed?

I know what you are thinking - the only person who is that interested in ME is my mother! Remember, this is not about YOU - it is about selling - it is about your customer. Don't EXPECT anyone to be that interested in you. But that doesn't mean you cannot be that interested and helpful to your customers. This changes the whole focus.

Now I am going to show YOU how to make any amount of money you want by using this theory. You see, I AM interested in your success - I want you to sell more and make more money.

Let's say you want to make $120,000 over the next 12 months. Usually you would say to yourself - "THIS IS MY GOAL - I WILL MAKE $120,000 IN COMMISSIONS DURING THE NEXT 12 MONTHS." By taking this approach, your focus is wrong.

Instead, try this... "I AM GOING TO GIVE $500 WORTH OF SERVICE EVERYDAY MONDAY THROUGH FRIDAY." Do you see the difference? Don't focus on the money - on what's in it for YOU - focus on GIVING THE SERVICE. The money will follow.

This is the New definition of selling - service. This definition is so new it is not even in the dictionary or thesaurus. The dictionary says selling means to persuade, or influence to a course of action. The thesaurus says selling is "barter, exchange, trade, traffic, and vend. Nowhere does it say selling is SERVICE. Nowhere does it say selling is helping your customers become more successful and make more money.

Let's put it another way. How much would someone PAY YOU to listen to your sales pitch? Zero - Right? Yet people pay thousands of dollars to consultants to ask questions - find out what they want - and help them get it. You can convey the same message to your customers.

23

The true purpose of a consultative salesperson is to find out what your customer wants and help them get it.

To accomplish this, you have to listen more than you talk. If you can get your customer to talk enough, they simply cannot disguise their real goals and real motives. They may try as hard as they can, but invariably they will "give themselves away." When they do - you have the key.

YOU KNOW WHAT THEY WANT!

Help them get it, and you will have captured the true meaning of being a sales professional.

When Henry Ford asked his customers what they needed, they said "A faster horse!"

If you're asking your customers what they need what will they tell you? "Cheaper prices!"

Henry Ford could see beyond the immediately obvious, look into the future and see a bigger picture. And that is what you must do to have record-breaking sales.

Let's go one step further. What do YOU need? If your answer is more sales, more customers and more money, you are giving the same answer as "A faster horse!" You are not looking at the bigger picture. You are not looking beyond the immediately obvious. You are not focusing on what will create your increased sales.

What you really need is to put tons of extra value in every product and service you offer.

And exactly how do you do that? By improving the level of service that is included with your price. Because when all things are equal, which is most of the time, the difference will be in the extra personal service you provide.

So what you really need is not a faster horse or cheaper prices. You need to be MOTIVATED to improve your service to your customers. And what could be newer and more welcome to your customers than a motivated, excited salesperson delivering exceptional service? It has been missing for the past several years. Everyone has been taking their customers for granted. Ho Hum! selling is dead, and if you are still delivering it, you too will be gone.

Instead of saying I need more sales, more customers and more money, try saying I need to GIVE more. I need to give my customers an enthusiastic attitude of service, more appreciation, more attention, and more action!

6. You're not excited

How about showing a little passion for what you do? There is just too much ho-hum selling going on today. There are too many salespeople who just don't get the fact that enthusiasm is contagious and as a salesperson, you have to infect everyone with a good dose of excitement.

How do you get jacked up?

Here's how to get UN-jacked. Tell yourself you are a loser. Tell yourself you hate what you do. Tell yourself you will never make the sale. Tell yourself your company sucks. Tell yourself you never got any of the breaks. Tell yourself the competition is ruthless. Tell yourself that everybody buys on price. Tell yourself that your sales territory is saturated and there is no business.

Do you know what ninety-five percent of everyone in prison were told over and over again as they were growing up: "You are going to end up in prison someday?" Think about it. Over and over again they were told they were going to end up in prison someday. What if they were told something different? What if they were told over and over again that they might be in a little trouble right now, but they will get past it? What if they were told that they were going to grow up and be successful? Would that make a difference? The stuff you put in your mind is the what controls your actions. So to get jacked up you have to put things in your mind that will get you excited and passionate about what you do for a living.

Put this affirmation in your mind. Carry it around with you and watch the difference...

(READ THIS LIKE YOU MEAN IT!) I am excited! I stay focused on all the good things I have to be excited about. I am excited about my career, my opportunities, and my challenges. My excitement drives me to do everything with energy and enthusiasm. My mind is focused fully on what I am doing and I am able to get things done by telling myself to "DO IT NOW". I am excited and act enthusiastic and everyone around me catches it. Every time I see someone I know or meet someone new I am excited and enthusiastic about seeing them. By being enthusiastic, excited and full of energy I am a more valuable person. Energy and enthusiasm guarantee my success as a highly paid professional sales person. Energy, passion, and enthusiasm will attract customers and sales to me. This energy will be like a magnet and attract bigger customers and larger commissions to me. I am going to give everything I have to everything I do.

Don't be a daydreamer. Don't wish you were somewhere else doing something different. Life is what it is. For whatever reason, you are where you are right now, so you have to deal with it. Keep this quote on your dashboard: "My job is not to see what lies dimly at a distance, but to do what lies clearly at hand!" That means there is no getting around it... you have to make the prospecting call, send the email, mail the letter, take care of the follow-up and keep going.

Forget about whether you feel like it or not. Actions come before feelings. ACT enthusiastic, and your feelings will follow. If you wait until you FEEL jacked up, you will be like the woman sitting on the park bench who turned into a skeleton waiting for the perfect man. It ain't gonna happen!

Here is another way to stay excited about what you are doing. Make training a DAILY part of your schedule. Spend time EVERYDAY learning something new about your business. Get excited about bringing news and information to your customers. In other words, start selling like you mean business. There is no excuse not to! Don't think it is up to the company to train you. It is up to you. Take responsibility. Invest in yourself. Read a book, take a course, listen to a motivational CD, read your marketing product sheets.

The bottom line. Learn something new today. Get your butt out there and make something happen. Call someone. Go visit a customer and bring them a new idea. Stop whining. No one said it was going to be easy! Your customers need help making good decisions. Go help them make the decision to buy from you by being excited, enthusiastic and jacked up! Let them know you really want their business!

7. You're a spectator not a doer

Over the years I have bought and sold several rental properties. One of my recent houses needed some yard work done. The backyard sloped towards the house and caused a water problem. I was going to build a deck, but first I needed to work on solving the water problem.

I started with a shovel. That lasted about 15 minutes. I knew there had to be a better way, so I headed to the equipment rental company.

After I arrived and looked over the options, I decided on a Bobcat. A Bobcat is a small tractor with a bucket on the front that scoops up the dirt. The person renting me the equipment asked if I knew how to operate it. I said "of course" thinking to myself "how hard can it be?" I hooked it up to my truck and headed home.

I pulled up behind my house, sat in the bobcat seat and prepared to pull it off the trailer. I started the engine, let out the clutch and lost control. It jerked ahead and by the time I figured how to stop it I had run into the gas meter and caused a gas leak. I immediately called the gas company, and they were there in a matter of minutes to fix it.

I got back on the Bobcat, and as I was turning around, I lost control again and destroyed two sections of my fence.

As soon as I started digging my wife opened the door and said the TV cable was out.   told her to call the cable company, and she said the phone didn't work. The only thing I didn't damage was the water main.

Twice during the day my neighbor, who is about 85 years old, walked over, looked at what I was doing, shook his head and walked away. At this point, I really didn't need any criticism.

At the end of the day – after 8 hours - my yard sloped the right way. I was putting the Bobcat back on the trailer when my neighbor came over. I was expecting him to tell me I was crazy. Instead, he said something that turned out to be the best compliment I have ever received. He said there are two kinds of people in the world. There are "spectators," and there are "doers." And then he walked away.

I have been selling my whole life, and I know hundreds of selling techniques. But there is only one thing that will make you any money in the selling profession: you have to take action.

In a recent study about why CEO's fail (based on researching about 30 CEO's who had failed in the last 10 years) one of the most interesting things discovered was that once a failed CEO resigned, many of the organizations quickly rebounded under a new CEO. It would seem the CEO was the difference. However, the study came to a fairly simple conclusion. CEO's don't fail due to lack of strategy or a grand vision. They fail in execution: They simply don't take action.

The same is true of sales professionals and their account relationships. A colleague of mine was recently doing interviews for a client to determine why some customers switched to the competition and others hadn't. Many of the salespeople who lost the accounts made reference to problems with the product, delivery, service, etc. My colleague's investigation showed the only common denominator was not the problems, but whether or not the salesperson took action to solve the problems.

Are you a spectator or a doer? Someone who watches or takes action?

8. You lack self confidence

There were about 45 salespeople in the meeting, and I was presenting them with one of my products, a hot dog. It was not a new product, but it was new to them. After everyone was just about finished sampling the hot dog, everyone seemed sold on the product. Then, all of a sudden, someone said, "Man, these hot dogs are really salty!" Pretty soon everyone agreed they were salty. I knew the salty hot dogs would never sell, so I had to act fast.

told them that I would arrange to have the hot dogs picked up from their warehouse and send them another order that would be reformulated with less salt. Two weeks later I was again at the sales meeting presenting the same salespeople with the reformulated hot dogs. Everyone agreed that they were much better. The formula with slightly less salt was a big improvement. We had a great introductory offer for their customers, and we sold tons of hot dogs. Everyone appreciated the extra effort I went to in order to give them the hot dog that they really wanted.

Here's the problem. I had the hot dogs picked up, put back in my warehouse, and two weeks later shipped the

EXACT SAME HOT DOGS BACK TO THEM! Do you really think a company that was making millions of pounds of hot dogs every day with hundreds of thousands of customers all over the world who were very happy with the product would change the formula because one guy in a sales meeting said they were salty?

No way. And besides, they were not salty, they tasted great. But I had to make them think that I was able to have the hot dog reformulated. One guy out of the 45 salespeople made an unthinking, uneducated comment, and pretty soon, the other 44 "sheep" believed him and started complaining about the salt content!

Now I have a really tough question for you. Are you one of the "sheep" who listens to someone on CNN and let them tell you that business is down, that no one is buying, that the hot dogs are salty? Are you one of the sheep who believes that politicians can create a cure-all for the economy? Are you one of the sheep who let other people tell you what and how to think while they knock your product and destroy your confidence? Or are you a confident enough salesperson who has the guts to stand up and go into psychological warfare with yourself and your customers and be part of the solution rather than part of the problem?

If you stick with any prediction long enough, it will happen. The media is unrelenting in its attempt to manufacture an actual recession, or at least convince people there is one. If you hear it from CNN, FOX, and MSNBC every single day, you will believe it. It is up to you to contradict the loud voices of gloom and doom telling your customers to lock up their money in fear. Money moves around, changes hands and gravitates to the person with an attitude for attracting it.

I didn't think the hot dogs were salty. I thought they tasted great. I wasn't about to let ONE uneducated salesperson spoil my business!

9. You can't handle rejection

You are probably being asked to make more sales calls, and you are having a problem. Here's why: More calls will result in more rejection.

Before I give you my technique for handling rejection, let me share with you a comment I received some time ago when I published the following information in a magazine article.

"I just read your article, Handling Rejection - Understand Why. Wow! I started my new business a couple of months ago. I refined my business plan, got leads, did a direct mailing, then I was frozen at the follow-up call. I didn't have cold calling or follow up call experience. Your article describes exactly how I feel, and it has given me the confidence to act like I now have the right to place that call. Thank you for writing it. I really enjoyed it. And you probably made me lots of money because now I'm going to make my calls."

The reason the comment is so important is to let you know that you are not alone. Everybody in sales gets that FEELING. You know the one I'm talking about. If you don't, it's only because you haven't been in sales long enough to make your first call. You are still under the delusion that everyone wants to see you and buy from you.

Here is the biggest reason you don't make the call in the first place:

You are worried about what they will think of you if you are unable to answer a tough question they might ask, or overcome an objection.

Here's a secret - they don't think about you.

Most people spend 98% of their time thinking about themselves. In the 2% of time left over, there is not much room to squeeze you in.

It has always been amazing to me how some people can let negative thoughts or comments occupy so much space in their mind. Some people let these thoughts freeze their activities and kill their career in sales. Every thought you carry around and dwell on should be paying rent for taking up space in your mind!

I am always impressed with people who have conquered their fear of rejection. I am much more impressed with them then I am the people who happen to stumble onto a big sale. I am always looking for them because I am so eager to learn how they do it.

Instead of letting them upset you why not just say to yourself: "That person has such a closed mind he won't even listen to me and with that kind of an attitude his business will probably go belly up because of his lack of interest in anything new! I'd better have these two young men send up a prayer for him because he is going to need more help then I can possibly give him anyway!!"

What just happened? YOU rejected HIM!

And THERE LIES THE KEY TO YOUR SUCCESS.

If your closing ratio for opening new customers is 1 out of every 10 here is what you have to do: Line up 10 calls with the idea that 9 will tell you to get lost! Nine of them are going to try to humiliate you. Nine of them are going to try and make you fail.

It's really a good thing for us in sales that there are a lot of dumb bunnies out there anyway.

Why?

Because they help the sales profession from becoming overcrowded. Let the other professions lock themselves in an office from 8 to 5 and quiver every time the boss walks by. Let the willy-nilly wimps take care of all those mundane activities. Let the timid non-assertive people who wake up every day in fear of their job hope and pray there is someone out there who knows how to CREATE BUSINESS. SOMEONE WHO KNOWS THAT BEING REJECTED IS PART OF THE GAME.

10. You don't have "GUTS"

I looked the word "guts" up in the thesaurus - here's what came back - courage, dauntlessness, heart, mettle, moxie, pluck, resolution, spirit, backbone, grit, intestinal fortitude, nerve, spunk! Put THAT list next to the phone or on the dashboard because THAT DESCRIBES YOU!

When somebody rejects you just say this:

"Two words for you buddy - thank you!" You are simply that much closer to finding a REAL customer.

The bigger the stakes, the bigger the chance for rejection. If you were playing in the Super Bowl and your team lost because YOU fumbled the ball THAT would be the ultimate rejection. How many millions of people would be rejecting you? Without taking that risk of rejection, you lose before you even start. You will never be in the Super Bowl of Sales.

Nobody likes rejection. It's natural to feel some disappointment when you hear someone say "no."

The issue is how you deal with that rejection. When you hear no it means you are doing your job.

The issue of rejection is not what the prospect or customer thinks of you, but what you think of yourself. Another important part of dealing with rejection is understanding why they rejected you.

Here is what I mean.

The reason may have to do with timing - at this particular moment in time, as you are making your sales call, they may be perfectly happy with their current vendor. They may have just had a fight with their spouse, and you happen to be the first one they talk to. They may not have had anything to eat all day, and it is affecting their mood. They may have just been turned down for a promotion - or a loan - or a new job. They may have just had to fire one of their employees. All these things have nothing to do with you.

You have to train your mind to respond to rejection with enthusiasm.

I sold insurance many years ago, and part of the training program was to go into a small office and make 10 cold phone calls. The phone was wired with speakers so the rest of the trainees could sit in the adjoining room and listen to the conversations. After you made your phone calls, you would be critiqued by your colleagues. That was easy. The hard part is when you are by yourself sitting in your car waiting for your appointment time, or when you are sitting alone at your desk in your home office and have to make the call. THAT is when it strikes.

A friend told me about a company where he applied for a job. The company sold something OTHER than vacuum cleaners. They sold computers. Yet, as part of his job qualification program, he had to sit in a room with a telephone and phone book, call 100 people at random and try to get an appointment to do a vacuum cleaner demonstration. Over half of the applicants would quit before they made it to 50 calls.

This fear of rejection could be costing you a lot of money if you are not making calls because of it.

How do you overcome this fear of approaching someone? Here's what you have to do even if you don't feel like it - you have to ask.

The bottom line of selling is to ask for your customer's or prospect's business. Don't be afraid to do just that. Don't be embarrassed to ask for what you want. Don't fear rejection. Don't worry about making the customer angry.

Don't be immobilized by your own timidity. Don't have negative thoughts that will set you up for failure.

Instead, say to yourself... "I love what I do - I love to sel I am in the right place at the right time. I have nothing to lose and everything to gain by making the call and asking for the business."

Selling is really simple. Selling is asking enough people to buy your products and services. Selling is weeding out all the ones that don't "get it." All you have to do is ask enough people to buy your products and services, and SOMEONE WILL BUY! If you don't make the request the customer is already ahead - you've made things easy for them! You've eliminated the possibility that they might actually say yes.

Don't let fear of rejection keep you from making the call. Approach each prospect with the idea that you are qualifying THEM. Do they qualify to buy from ME? Do they have the means to pay for what I'm selling? Are they smart enough to realize the value of what I am offering? Are they worth the investment of my valuable time? Is there enough business on the table for me to spend time and money to get my share?

When calling on a new prospect, those are the questions you want answered. When you make a prospect call or a cold call, there is always a certain amount of hesitation because the pressure is on YOU to make a presentation. Forget about making a presentation. Go in with the attitude that you are QUALIFYING THEM. If they don't measure up THEY are the poor souls that miss out! They are the ones that lose.

Read this next sentence carefully. To reduce call hesitation when calling on a prospect, make the call with the idea that you are qualifying the prospect and you can reject THEM if they don't measure up. Now you have the power. You have the power of rejection. You don't like to be rejected. So why give anyone the power to reject you? You are simply making the call to INVESTIGATE. You are there to get the FACTS ABOUT THEM. What you have to sell may be way beyond their understanding. It may be way over their head. To find out, you have to make the call and do the interview.

There is a certain fear you feel when trying to sell something to a stranger. But now you are not trying to sell on that initial contact. You are eliminating unqualified prospects. Don't let fear of rejection keep you from picking up the phone and making the call. You - your products - your services - are the answer to their prayers.

Are they good enough to do business with YOU!

11. You give up too soon

When you face an impossible task, it should not stop you, it should bring out the best in you.

Do you lack the necessary PERSISTENCE to keep going in spite of the opposition? If your answer is yes, NOW is the time to change your attitude!

Colonel Sanders owned a restaurant that seated 142 people in Corbin, Kentucky, where he perfected his secret blend of 11 herbs and spices and the basic cooking technique that is still used today.

In 1950 a new interstate highway was planned to bypass the town of Corbin. Seeing an end to his business, the Colonel closed his restaurant and auctioned off his equipment. After paying his bills, he was broke at the age of 65. He was reduced to living on his $105 Social Security checks.

Confident of the quality of his fried chicken, the Colonel devoted himself to the chicken franchising business that he started in 1952. He traveled across the country by car visiting thousands of restaurants, cooking batches of chicken for the owners and their employees. If the reaction was favorable, he entered into a handshake agreement on a deal that stipulated a payment to him of a nickel for each chicken the restaurant sold.

By 1964, Colonel Sanders had 600 franchised outlets for his chicken in the United States and Canada. That year, he sold his interest in the company for $2 million to a group of investors. The Colonel remained a public spokesman for the company until he died in 1980. In 1976, an independent survey ranked the Colonel as the world's second most recognizable celebrity.

What does Colonel Sanders have to do with you?

Everything!

I don't care how good a salesperson you are, it is unlikely that you will ever sell more than 2 out of every 10 prospects on your first call. That is as certain as the sun coming up in the east every morning. It is just the way selling is.

It took Colonel Sanders 12 years to sell 600 people on his "nickel a chicken" concept. Let's do the math.

That is 50 sales per year or one per week. To sell one per week, he would have to make 5 presentations per week. Remember, that's the most anybody can sell on their first call - 20%. If you happen to have a run on sales and sell 30%, you will have a dry spell where you sell only 10%.

Five presentations per week equal 250 per year. Over a 12 year period that is a whopping 3,000 presentations!

And remember, he did this from age 65 to 77.

What do you think was going through his mind when 4 out of 5, or 8 out of 10 prospects turned him down? Knowing people the way I do, I'm sure some thought he was a joke, some told him to get lost, some told him he couldn't be serious. "A N CKLE A CHICKEN? WHERE DID YOU EVER COME UP W TH A CRAZY IDEA LIKE THAT?"

Do you think The Colonel felt insecure and worried about what he was trying to do? Do you think that when he was alone at night in his hotel in some strange town with his cooking equipment and spices smelling up his hotel room, he had doubts about being able to get people to pay him as agreed?

I think you know the answer. And that brings us to you.

One of the hardest things to overcome is the feeling of insecurity when you are selling on commission for a living. Without the security of a guaranteed income, your thoughts are continually interrupted by fears of failure, rejection and "what people will think if I don't make it."

This is serious for the person going through it. If you are on commission and only get paid when you make a sale, or in your own business and are totally responsible for earning an income, it is easy to have visions of not being able to pay your expenses. And sometimes you CAN'T pay your expenses, and you have to deal with that as well.

The obvious solution most people will give you is to control your attitude - easy to say and does not really offer a solution. A positive attitude is the end result you are trying to achieve.

Many short-term programs give you temporary relief such as self-talk, repeating affirmations and listening to motivation tapes. These activities are helpful; however, they are not dealing with the core of the problem.

The question is; how do you keep moving forward with a positive attitude when you feel insecure and unsure of yourself? This insecure feeling causes you to look into the future with apprehension no matter how hard you try to think positive. You still see negative results from the effort you are putting forth today.

You are not convinced that if you do the right things over and over again, you will achieve the results you want. You can try affirmations by saying over and over to yourself, "I will make the sale," "I will get the new account" and still end up with negative results. Why? Because even as you say the words and visualize the results, you don't really expect it to happen!   You don't get what you want, what you wish for, what you think about, what you visualize or what you affirm. You get what you expect.

12. You don't expect it to happen

Let's say you wanted to have a backup cash reserve of $25,000 in the bank. You could affirm to yourself "I have a bank account with $25,000 in it." You could write it down as a "written goal." You could think "positive" about it. And still – nothing happens.

Why?   Because you really don't expect it to happen! You don't BELIEVE. You might feel good about it for a short time. But after a few weeks, it will fade away. Reality will overtake you, and you will file your $25,000 bank account idea away as a wish or a daydream or "it would be nice."

You have also reinforced the concept that affirmations, goal setting, positive thinking, and visualization don't work.   The next time you try to get something you want it becomes even more difficult because you not only have to overcome your current feelings of doubt and fear – you also have to deal with your past. "I've tried this before – it didn't work out – but I'll give it another shot." Then, no matter how hard you try, deep down inside you don't really expect it to happen and you are right - It doesn't.

You get what you expect. Nothing more - nothing less. If you want to increase your sales, you have to really EXPECT IT TO HAPPEN.

There is only ONE THING that builds expectations – ACTION – doing something productive.

  think the secret Colonel Sanders used to overcome the feeling of insecurity that every human being feels was his DECISION TO KEEP GOING. Every morning he got up and presented his "nickel a chicken" concept to another restaurant. AND 4 OUT OF 5 TOLD HIM TO GET LOST!

There is a big lesson that Colonel Sanders taught us. The Colonel's secret to sales is action. Picking up the phone and making the call, asking for the order at the price you want, writing the letter, or sending a follow-up card.

That is the secret spice of success - action.

13. You believe in superstitions

For the past several years I believed that I could not sell any of my sales training programs and keynote talks during July and August.

"They," said everyone is on vacation. "They," said no one has sales meetings in the hot July and August months.

I decided to challenge my thinking and see if there really is such a thing as the "summer slump."

I made extra calls and put in a little extra effort. Low and behold - I made a sale. Then another and another. It turned out that July and August were my best months of the year!

I couldn't stop there. I looked in my history books to see what was done during the hot "Dog days of summer."

Here is what I found...

The heat of southern Spain did not force Columbus to wait until "Labor Day." He sailed July 22nd!

George Washington did not retire to the shade of Mount Vernon when it got hot. He took active command of the Continental Army on July 3rd!

During the dog days of JULY and AUGUST, the Puritans set sail for the new world!

Our forefathers met and signed the Declaration of Independence!

Singer sold his first sewing machine...

The first section of the Atlantic cable was laid...

Lincoln began his debates with Douglas in the July heat of the Illinois prairies...

The first oil was struck at Titusville...

Meade defeated the Confederate Army at Gettysburg in July...

The first streetcar line was operated in this country...

Europe began the greatest war in history...

The French Revolution was started in July...

The first locomotive steam train chugged out of a Baltimore station for the West - in July...

July and August were the "golden days" for the forerunners of the modern sales representative - with everything in the back end of their buggies from lightning rods to chewing tobacco.

Forty-two thousand gold seekers crossed Death Valley to California in 1850 when the temperature hung around 130 degrees... in July and August!

"Wait until after Labor Day!" "They," say.

"There is not any business now!"

"No use killing oneself in this weather - nobody buys until fall!"

The next time the friendly competitive salesperson edges over to you in the lobby and admits there is nothing doing until after Labor Day, encourage him or her in this delusion.

AND THEN SLIP OUT AND MAKE THE BIGGEST SALES OF THE YEAR - BEFORE LABOR DAY!

The bottom line - DO NOT BELIEVE IN SUPERSTITIONS! SELL 52 WEEKS A YEAR!

14. You don't use your GPS

As I write this, I am in Columbus Ohio and just took my rental car back. I didn't have to worry about how to find my way around because I had a GPS (Global Positioning System) telling me where to go. All I had to do was put in my destination and, like magic, I was given step by step detailed instructions on where to go.

Here's what I was thinking. "Wouldn't it be great if I had a GPS that would guide me towards my goal? I could program in my goal and get minute to minute feedback telling me if I am on course, or if I need to change direction or change my activities."

You guessed it.

You and I do have a GPS already installed. It just has to be programmed. Once you enter your destination, you will be guided with surgical precision. Here is the biggest problem with our GPS. We don't have confidence that it will actually work. We seem to have more confidence in a GPS that is placed on the dashboard than the one place between our ears!

So the first part of the programming process is to choose a specific destination. It has to be specific. You can't program a GPS to head south. You have to enter an address, or at least a city. It can't be a destination that is unreachable or unclear.

The input must be realistic, measurable, obtainable and most important, specific. You have either reached your destination, or you have not. There is no gray area. As soon as you reach it, you can enter your next destination.

And be sure to program your GPS with ACTIVITY goals. You will never know if you will sell any single person, so the goal of "open 2 new accounts" will never work. Instead, program the activities it will take to get 2 new accounts. "Carefully select 10 new prospects and start contacting them every week until 2 or more place an order." Your GPS will respond without any problem.

Your GPS will let you know if you are off course by planting some guilt and self-doubt if you DON'T keep your promise to yourself. It becomes easier to make the 10 extra calls than to keep hearing your GPS in the background telling you that you are a loser! (That's part of your guidance system). If you MAKE the 10 extra calls, your confidence and self-esteem will be higher.

It makes sense that if you don't know where you want to go, or what you want to accomplish, you won't ever establish a working plan of action. The purpose of the GPS is to keep bringing you back on track. Every day things happen to really mess up the plan. But with your GPS destination, you keep coming back on track.

You have to keep entering your GPS data! According to everything I have ever read about goal setting it all seems to communicate this message: You have to rewrite your goal every day. So it is like a GPS. Every morning sit down and write your goal and your list. Your built is GPS will be working in the background to get you there.

Without a goal it is like a trip I took to Quebec. Everything was in French. Everything! I couldn't read a single road sign. Had I not had my GPS I would have been completely lost. However, all I had to do was enter the address of the hotel I was heading to, and presto, step by step instructions were given to me.

What is the address you want to end up at? Write it down. Give your mind a clear picture of what it looks like and presto! Step by step instructions will come to you almost like magic.

15. You're filled with uncertainty

How would you like to have an insurance policy that was going to guarantee your success in sales? I have that policy for you. It will guarantee success and remove all the "uncertainty" about selling.

Here it is.

The next time you become jittery because selling is such a risky business, consider this: The risk that an insurance company takes on one individual policyholder is the most unpredictable thing in the world.

What could be riskier than trying to guess when one certain individual is going to have an accident or become sick, or how long he or she is going to live?

Yet the insurance business itself is the most stable in the country, the safest investment anyone can make-the nearest thing to a "sure thing" in the way of guaranteed returns to investors.

The risk an insurance company takes on one individual policyholder is tremendous, yet the risk involved in 100,000 policyholders is so predictable it can be figured to the fourth decimal point.

Whether or not you will sell any single prospect is unpredictable.

But do as the insurance companies do; "spread the risk" by making a sufficient number of presentations.

By making a certain number of presentations, you can adopt the attitude that "I've got nothing to lose" before making a call, instead of telling yourself, "Everything depends on this," you can now tell yourself that "EVERYTHING DOES NOT DEPEND ON THIS."

You can strike out occasionally and still hit more home runs than anyone else on the team. Say to yourself, "If I don't call on this customer and ask for the order, the sale is lost anyway. If I call on him or her and fail, I won't be any worse off than I am right now, so I have nothing to lose."

 When you strike out a few times and keep going you get over the "fear of failure." Spread the risk like the insurance companies do, broaden your customer base and make more contacts.

For many salespeople marketing seems to be a separate division of the company with its own, unrelated agenda.

However, marketing strategies can be used individually to help build your business.

The first step in marketing is to identify your target customer and determine how many customers it will take to maintain your business. Here's what I mean, using examples from different industries.

Let's say you wanted to sell residential real estate for a living. You would need to stake out an area that has a minimum of 500 houses. If you began a systematic schedule of contacting these 500 homeowners on a monthly basis, some in person, some on the phone, some by mail, there would be enough houses bought and sold each year to make a living.

Another good example is insurance. You would have to have a list of one thousand households and contact them on a regular basis. There would be enough insurance needs to earn a living. Both examples depend, of course, on your ability to outsell the competition.

Even a nursing home with one hundred beds has to have them filled with residents. If they have ten empty beds for any length of time, their expenses go up, and their profits go down.

A hospital is in a similar situation. The success of their marketing is measured by their "occupancy rate." The next time you call on a hospital ask what their occupancy rate is and you will be surprised at how quickly they can give you the percentage.

A manufacturer looking for national distribution needs 200 distributors. Fifty for each quarter of the country. This will result in enough coverage to sell in every corner of the US.

Looking at a restaurant's business from a marketing perspective can also be measured with mathematical precision. A restaurant needing to sell a thousand meals each week to take in enough money to pay all their expenses needs a customer base of five thousand. A marketing "rule of thumb" for a restaurant is to take one week's business and multiply it times five. Restaurant customers normally rotate their eating out so you would want to be sure that you had five thousand people "rotating" into your business at least once every five weeks.

What about a Distributor Sales Rep (DSR)? How many customers do you need and how much do you have to sell each account to make a living?

The average DSR sells a little over two million dollars each year, or $40,000 each week. The average order size in the industry is $500. That means to be "average" you would have to sell 80 accounts $500 every week. NOT A GOOD PLAN!

What if you double the order size to $1,000? That brings the number of accounts down to 40. Forty accounts purchasing $1,000 each week sounds better. However, you are still only "average."

Let's give it one more twist. Let's weed out the low margin price shoppers and carefully select 40 accounts that could buy at least $2,000 per week from you. Now you are investing your time and effort with prospects that will give you sales exceeding four million dollars per year.

It looks good on paper, as all marketing plans do. However, it is still up to you to make it happen the old-fashioned way, by selling.

16. You talk too much and don't listen

If you are not getting past first base with your customers, perhaps it's because you talk too much and don't get the needed information about your customers.

What are the biggest complaints customers have about salespeople?

Too pushy? Poor follow up? Lack of knowledge?

Those are the ones that are usually brought up when asking salespeople what they think. However, one of the biggest complaints is not surprising: we talk too much. One of the most challenging things for many salespeople to do is listening to their customers. The reason we talk too much is understandable. You called on the customer and asked for some of the r time. This sets up a professional expectation on the part of the buyer. "You asked for my time, now tell me why you want it."

The pressure then falls on the salesperson to deliver a presentation. This is the point in the selling process that separates the amateur from the professional. The rookie mistakenly believes that selling and talking are the same things. The professional knows that you cannot sell anything until you first understand what the customer wants. How can this be accomplished?

Instead of starting off the meeting talking about your products, services or company, start off by asking a few questions. "I am here to talk about how some of our services might be of benefit, however, before I start do you mind if I ask a few questions?"

The most compelling selling message you can deliver is not that you have something great to sell. It is "I understand what you are trying to accomplish." Find out what they want, where they are going and who they are.

Remember these famous words: "Whoever talks the most during a sales presentation ends up with the product."

Asking the "why" question. In buying or selling it is not always smart to be too decisive or knowledgeable. This is one of the classic strategies - it is well used by seasoned salespeople.

This strategy is used to draw you out with the aim of extracting more information from you. You are up against a smooth buyer when this is used against you.

You will get better answers if you are slow to understand. The trouble is that most of us want to look good. We find it hard to say, "I don't know" or "tell me that again."

An excellent example of asking for help: While I was sitting in a sales manager's office getting ready to go to lunch with him, his secretary announced that his 11:45 life insurance appointment was here. I volunteered to leave, but he said it would only take a few minutes and to stay put.

The young insurance man entered the office, handed the sales manager an application and said, "You don't want to buy any life insurance, do you?" That is considered the poorest choice of words a salesperson could ever se.

The sales manager couldn't believe what he was hearing. He sat the insurance man down and for 15 minutes lectured him on how to sell. He told him how to use features and benefits, family protection, cash build up, and education funds.

The sales manager said he was going to buy $250,000 additional coverage and began showing the young insurance man how to fill out the application. The sales manager handed the insurance salesman the completed application along with a deposit check and said, "Son, I hope you have learned never to use that opening question again?"

As the insurance man was leaving, his signed application and deposit check in hand, he turned to the sales manager and said, "Oh, I never use that line, unless I'm calling on a sales manager."

Customer surveys are basically useless because people only tell you what you want to hear. Here is a magic question that will reveal the true feelings of your customer: How can I make it better?

Q: How has our service been? A: It has been fine. Q: How can we make it better?

By using this additional question, you are able to extract the real information you need. With this information, you may be able to make changes or improvements before it's too late and you lose the customer to a more creative competitor.

You will get better answers if you are slow to understand. The trouble is that most of us want to look good. We find it hard to say, "I don't know" or "tell me that again."

17. You can't get new customers

"I forgot they were coming!"

"I wonder how long this is going to take."

"My production supervisor is on vacation."

"My office manager called in sick this morning!"

"YIKES! Look at all the stuff they have with them!"

"There are two of them - they will probably never stop talking."

"This is going to take forever - I've got to do something - fast."

"I see they have a price book - good - I know how to get rid of them."

"I'll get a price quote on something and tell them they are way too high.""

If you are having the door slammed in your face before you even have a chance to say hello - you may be doing it wrong.

Let me explain.

Why do you go to the office before an appointment and gather a ton of brochures, fill your briefcase with samples, get a complete product list, take your laptop, and ask someone else to go on the sales call with you?

Your first mistake is thinking that the potential customer is remotely interested in you or what you are selling. You mistakenly believe that they want to read your brochures (they don't), listen to your sales pitch (they have a hundred other things that are more pressing) and ask questions about you and your company (they really don't care). You mistakenly think that you are showing the importance you put on the appointment because there are two of you.

When they agreed to the appointment - you caught them at a weak moment. I am sure you have heard of "buyers remorse." Let me introduce you to a new concept – "agreeing to an appointment remorse." As soon as they hang up the phone, it starts - "Why did I agree to see that salesperson?"

Agreeing to an appointment is like buying on a credit card - easy to make the purchase - hard to pay off.

Something you said may have sparked a small interest during your initial phone conversation - that spark has long since gone out by the time you show up.

So the question is: Why do you bring all this stuff with you and why do you invite someone to go along? You might be thinking that the reason is to be prepared.

The answer is - you lack confidence. I know – that's tough to swallow – but it is the truth. Having all this stuff and bringing someone with you assures you that you will have something to talk about.

Here is a little-known secret about selling. Your job is not to talk, but to listen - not to present, but to ask questions.

The first thing you have to do is lower the prospects defenses. You do this by going alone and not taking anything, or anybody, with you. No computer, no brochures, no prices, not even a briefcase. This takes courage because most salespeople are taught that their job is to "show and tell." When you walk into an account "unarmed" and simply ask permission to ask a few questions, there is very little pressure on the buyer and even less on you.

As a professional, you have to evaluate the account to see if it will be profitable for you to invest your time with them. You have to position yourself to be on the offensive rather than the defensive when making a new account call. If you don't have your price book and someone wants to put you on the defensive by asking for a price – simply say "I don't know" and continue to ask questions about their business.

The process of calling on an account without a lot of baggage is similar to a visit to the dentist or doctor - you would want a complete examination before getting an operation or having a tooth pulled.

The first time you try it, you will feel "unprepared." That is a good sign - it means you are trying something new and at the brink of learning a new skill.

I would like to challenge you to make a few cold calls this week completely unarmed - not unprepared - just unarmed.

What are you going to talk about? You are not going to talk - you are going to ask questions.

18. You can't get attention

Sometimes you have to take a negative approach to get a positive response, sometimes you have to be creative to get someone's attention in the first place, and sometimes you have to really think outside the box to make people take notice.

Whenever I am on an airplane or in a crowd of strangers, I am asked what I do. According to the experts, you should have an "elevator speech" for these occasions. You should be able to tell people what you do by the time the elevator makes it from one floor to the next.

I designed a clever 30-second speech, and it really seemed to turn people off. As soon as I said I was a "sales trainer" I could see the expression on their face turn to panic. They immediately said they don't use sales trainers, or they have a company employee who does their sales training. They had a ready-made objection. So by following the advice of the experts, I was turning people off in less than 30 seconds.

Back to the drawing board. I took a different approach by thinking outside the box.

I created a "shock" effect, and I am now able to get people's interest and have some fun at the same time. Now, when they ask me what I do, here is what I say:

"I show people how to stay 4 steps ahead of the sheriff, would you like to know what those 4 steps are?" And they always say YES?

I give them four quick steps that would be applicable to them and ask which step would be most helpful. If they say "step 3" I give them a really good sound bite of information on step 3. I then get their business card and follow up with some more helpful information.

I am getting ready to do a 5,000-piece mailing and guess what will be on the envelope? You got it: "How to stay 4 steps ahead of the sheriff, would you like to know what the 4 steps are?"

When you are approaching a new account, think of your first few words as the sales copy on the envelope. The job of the sales copy is NOT to make the sale, but to get them to OPEN IT UP!

Keep in mind that if they don't open the envelope, the sale will NEVER be made! The same with your opening line. If you don't hit the right button the door of their mind doesn't open.

Here are some of the standard openers and my translation. If you are guilty, you might spend a little time creating something that works for you. Be easy on yourself, everyone has used them.

"I am sorry for interrupting."

Translation: I really don't amount to much - you are much more important than I am - you see I am just a doormat waiting for someone to wipe their feet on me.

"I know you are busy."

Translation: I really don't have any respect for you or your time - you are a busy and important person, and I am intruding in your day.

"I was in the neighborhood."

Translation: I am not very organized - I simply drift through my day from neighborhood to neighborhood making random calls on people and waste their time.

"Do you need anything?"

Translation. I am really not much of a, and I was wondering if there are any crumbs left over from a real salesperson who has been here.

"I wanted to stop by and introduce myself."

Translation. I am really not ambitious enough to have done some homework about you, so I guess I will tell you all about ME.

I think you get the point. Things are different out there today, so you have to be different, or they eat you alive.

Today's customers are being bombarded with an estimated 3,000 sales and marketing messages every day. How do you stand out and set yourself apart from the crowd? You have to hit them with a HUGE BENEFIT. A benefit that will have the same power as if you hit them between the eyes with a baseball bat!

19. You don't create demand

In Orlando, Florida, the visionary Walt Disney had a team of folks buy all the property he needed to build Disney World. They were able to keep everyone sworn to secrecy. As soon as the purchase became known and everyone found out what was going on, the property values went sky high.

If you want to sell hot dogs in New York City, you would have to buy a license. There are only a certain number of licenses available, which makes them increase in value. The current selling price for a hot dog cart license in New York City is between $350,000 and $500,000.

The same is true for a taxicab license.

The Los Angles Country Club was built in the 1950's at which time you could buy one of a thousand available memberships for $5,000. The standing price today is one million dollars.

You can see that people want what they can't have. When they can't have it, value is created.

How can this help you? Here is an example.

There is a Martial Arts company near my home, and my nephew is a member. When he first started going, he was getting a lot of individual attention. Being a member of the team was important. After one-year things started to change. The instructor wanted to go form 50 students to 150 students. He moved to a more expensive location, hired some help, and now spends most of his time chasing after new recruits to help pay for his increased overhead. He is actually making less money than he was with his original 50, many who have left.

What if he understood the concept of supply and demand?

What if he would have raised his price and limited his students to 50. The only way you could become a member would be by referral, and then you had to fill out an application and go through an interview process along with the parents. Interviews would be held only once per month on the second Tuesday from noon until 9:00 PM, by appointment.

What if, rather than answer his phone you heard a recording that said he was training his students and is unable to come to the phone because he didn't want to interrupt their focus and concentration.

What if all phone calls were returned at the end of the day by his wife (who works with him as his assistant) and find out what they wanted. If it were important enough, a phone appointment would be set up with the instructor.

This is the same strategy doctors, and dentists use to create a sense of being busy. They schedule appointment times close together and make you wait.

During your initial contact with a prospect, imply that you are only there to see if they qualify for you to spend time and energy helping them solve their problems.

20. You don't know what they want

Everyone in sales has been searching for a key which would magically unlock the door of the mind of every prospect we call on.

Here it is:

You and I, and every person we know live in a tomorrow! That tomorrow maybe a few hours off. It may be this afternoon or next week, a month, a year, or even ten years from now. Ninety percent of the excitement in the present is the imaginary picture we are constantly recreating in our minds of a tomorrow. It will always be a better tomorrow. We picture ourselves as happier then. We will be healthier, more comfortable, with less worries, with more leisure, with more money, with greater power... we will strangely be freed of the realities that make today far from satisfactory.

This attitude forms the texture of desire. It is at the base of the mind of every person who has lived in America for more than twenty-four hours. It is our national philosophy, our habitual trend of thought. We know we are going to be better off tomorrow than we are today.

Every waking hour our mind glides out of the present into the future, and we see ourselves as we will be tomorrow.

The business owner never likes the profit and loss statement of today... but tomorrow profits are going to climb! He or she pictures a new line of merchandise or menu item moving quickly at a greater profit.

Today the manager must work three nights a week to keep his or her desk clean, but they picture a tomorrow when this new computer will clean the desk at five o'clock, un-fatigued and with peace of mind. Tomorrow! We live most of it today. It is so much better than today. The person who sits across from you now is not thinking about themselves as they are now . . . They are building a mental picture of themselves as they will be tomorrow and tomorrow and tomorrow . . . with this or that added, which they are about to purchase ... which when acquired will make them much happier. They see themselves with more customers, with larger gross profits, lower labor costs and less taxes to pay.

Politicians. Successful politicians use this concept in every speech. They know that if they want to stay in office or be elected to office, they have to know what the people want and build it into every talk they give. They never like to talk about the past and very rarely address issues in the present, it's always the future. "I am your bridge to the 21st century". "Your door to the future."

Travel agency. A travel agency always gives you a clear vision of where you are going, never on the trip getting there. A seven-day cruise sales presentation shows you the fun you will have on board ship, all the food and entertainment you will enjoy. However, they neglect to tell you about the 7-hour flight to Puerto Rico where you meet the ship and the 4 hours you have to stand on the dock waiting in line.

Insurance companies. The insurance industries entire existence relies on selling you the future. When you buy insurance, you spend thousands of dollars and have nothing in return except a piece of paper. They present you with a mental picture of what would happen to your family if you were to die. They show you how many people reach old age without any money or retirement. They give examples of the high cost of going to the hospital for surgery. The insurance companies are experts at getting a piece of your future. This does not mean that it is good or bad, it simply is the way they sell their products and services.

Lawyers. A good lawyer is the true artist in the area of painting future pictures. They usually do it based on fear of loss. When you tell them about your concern, they paint a picture of gloom by blowing your problem up to the maximum. Then, of course, they tell you how much work it would be to take care of it and, with no guarantees, will represent you for a fee.

Credit cards. One of the single largest goals of most people today is to have the money to pay off their credit card balances. How did so many people get in this situation where the average married couple owes around
$25,000 in credit card bills. Once we look at the concept of appealing to someone's future, creating an impatience and a willingness to go in debt for things they didn't think they could live without, it is easy to understand why people borrow on their future. During the last 12 months over one million people filed personal bankruptcy to get out from under their debts.

Law enforcement. Law enforcement is similar to the way the lawyers use this powerful concept. The worst thing that could happen to an individual is to have their future taken away from them.

21. You exaggerate benefits

Don't let them make the mistake that many salespeople make. This huge mistake is exaggerating. When you are selling an idea or trying to convince someone of something, you more than likely over exaggerate your claims.

To get your idea across you may feel you have to use such overworked phrases as:

"We are number one..."

"We are the best in the business..."

"You can save big money with us..."

As soon as one of these statements is made a red flag goes up in the buyer's mind. In your opening statement, you have just "unsold" yourself. The buyer, customer or person you are trying to convince knows immediately that you are stretching the truth. The buyer (I refer to anyone you are trying to get to buy into your idea, product or service as a "buyer") has three questions:

1. "So what?"

2. "What's in it for me?"

3. "Can you prove it?"

Instead of using the above-overworked phrases you should use facts, figures, and examples in your presentation to justify your statements. These facts make the buyer willing to accept you and your offer. Your goal is to weave the facts into the conversation that makes the buyer understand the LEGITIMACY of what you are saying.

Like a shrewd attorney, you want to present your facts in the strongest possible light. For example: "Our program will increase your profits by 6% - here is how." Or "This product line will cut your labor cost by 3% - I have the facts right here to prove what I am saying." Or "This new marketing system will increase your sales by at least 5% - let me show you what I mean."

An idea is sold not necessarily when you go into your close, but when the buyer agrees with your statements - and that is what you are looking for - buyer commitment.

Your goal is to weave the facts into the conversation that makes the buyer understand the LEGITIMACY of what you are saying.

22. You don't present value

I am going to make this crystal clear. When you finish reading this, you should easily be able to switch your customer from buying on price to buying on value.

Here are some examples that should shift your thinking and show you how to shift the thinking of your customer.

If you have $100 to spend on dinner to celebrate your kids birthday, what are you going to look for? The best value for your money.

If you have $400 in your budget for a monthly car payment, what are you going to look for? The most car for your payment.

If you have been pre-qualified by the bank to buy a $150,000 house, what are you going to look for? The most house for your money.

If you have 4 kids and a grocery budget of $250 a week, what are you going to look for? The most value for your money.

If you have decided that you are going to spend $2,000 on a new flat screen TV, what are you going to look for? The most TV for your $2,000.

OK, I know what you are thinking. How can you use this to make the sale instead of cutting the price?

Here is how to make the shift in thinking.

You're selling to a restaurant owner. Here is what you say: "You are spending $5,000 per week for your food, so your goal is to get the most value and the highest quality for your $5,000 weekly investment, is that correct? That is why we don't simply throw out prices and try to beat everyone. We take your budget and give you the highest value for your investment. For example, our service, our quality, our in-stock items, etc.

You're selling staffing services. Here is what you say: "You are paying $18.00 per hour for an employee, so your goal is to get the most value for your $18.00 per hour investment, is that correct? That is why we don't simply try to beat everyone's hourly price. We take your budget and give you the highest value for your investment. For example, here are 57 services we can offer that makes us the best value for your money.

You're selling a training and coaching program. Here is what you say: "I am sure you will agree, $200 per month per person is a very reasonable investment for training and coaching, especially with the results you will get? Here is why our program delivers so much more value for your investment than anything else available: You can continue until your sales are up to where they need to be. Plus you can miss a session and easily make it up. Plus we can become your ongoing training partner. Plus our training is very interactive - NOT a lecture series! Plus we address your individual selling roadblocks and find solutions! Plus you can quit anytime if you are not happy and your payments stop! Plus you can start RIGHT NOW - NO WAITING - GET IMMEDIATE RESULTS! Plus you can have confidence in our results because we are experts - all we do is sales training! That is more value than any other program available, especially for the small monthly investment, don't you agree?"

You're selling a house. Here is what you say: "I am sure you will agree, the payment on this house is $1,227 per month including taxes and insurance is a stretch. You may be able to find a house with a smaller payment, but look at this street, look at this neighborhood, look at this backyard, how about this great deck, and this fireplace, and these appliances, and the home owner's warranty, and the association benefits, etc."

You are selling a car. Here is what you say: "What is the payment or price range you are looking for? $400 per month. Then our goal is to find you the best value for your investment, let's start with this one I have right here. It not only has a huge rebate, all the great features, but we have marked it down as well. With all this, you are actually getting a $600 per month car for a $400 per month investment."

1. You first ask: "How much are you already spending, or how much are you willing to spend, or how much do you have in your budget?"

2. You then ask: "I assume your goal is to get the most value for your investment, is that correct?

3. Your presentation is helping them make the best decision by showing how much value they will get when they buy from you?

The purpose of your presentation is to justify your prices before they become an objection.

23. You let objections stop you

Do any of these sound familiar?

I have too many suppliers already.

I really don't like your company.

We've been doing all right without you.

I'm tied up in a supplier contract.

I'm happy with my present supplier.

You don't carry a full line.

'm not interested at this time.

See me in a couple of months.

I hear your company is having problems.

Business is down.

Why will someone continue to buy from a salesperson when it is obvious, they are not happy with the service, price or quality? The reason is that the buyer is comfortable dealing with the salesperson and company he or she is buying from. To make a change requires assurances that you will be able to handle their business. Many times in the buyer's mind it is easier to stay with their current supplier even if the prices and delivery are not exactly as they would like. That is why they have at least five objections that you must overcome before they feel sure enough to give you their business.

The best response to smoke screen objections is to be sincerely glad they brought it up. When answering "smoke screen" objections, the normal response is to agree with the objection. However, the best response is to say "I'm glad you brought that up!" And then ask a question.

This is a non-confrontational approach. When you do it sincerely, you will come across with real concern for your customer.

How would you handle these common objections? I have too many suppliers already. I really don't like your company. We've been doing all right without you. I'm tied up in supplier contract. I'm happy with my present supplier. You don't carry a full line. I'm not interested at this time. See me in a couple of months. I hear your company is having problems. Business is down.

When answering these "smoke screen" objections, the normal response is to agree with the objection. However, an excellent response is to say, "I'm glad you brought that up!" And then ask a question. For example:

"I don't like your company." Response: "I'm glad you brought that up. It sounds to me like someone must have done something in the past and it is Important that we get honest feedback about our products and services. What exactly is it that you don't like about our company?"

"I have too many suppliers already." Response: "I'm glad you brought that up. That certainly can be a problem, how many are too many?" "I may be able to help you consolidate," etc.

"You don't carry the items I need." Response: "I'm glad you brought that up. Would you mind telling me which items you are referring to?"

Often, we can get the prospect to answer his own objection or to admit that it is not a valid objection. To let the prospect answer his own objection, you just let them talk. Maybe he will answer his own objection. In any event, he will lower his blood pressure. You may say, for example, "I am interested in why you say that, Mr. Smith. I wish you would explain it to me more fully." You may merely ask him, "Why do you believe that?" If, as so often happens, the objection is not a valid one and the prospect has at best only a half-baked idea of what he is talking about, he will usually flounder around a while and end by admitting that the matter is of no importance.

When answering "smoke screen" objections, the normal response is to agree with the objection. However, the best response is to say "I'm glad you brought that up!" And then ask a question.

The reason salespeople hesitate to ask for what they want is fear of rejection.

Don't fear rejection.

Don't worry about making the customer angry.

Don't be immobilized by your own timidity.

Don't have negative thoughts that will set you up for failure.

"They'll never give up their current supplier and buy from me, so there's no point in even asking."

If you don't make the request, the customer is already ahead!

You've made things easy for them! They made the pitch, and you bought it!

You've eliminated the possibility that they might say yes or agree to a compromise solution that is equally desirable.

If you are dealing with a person who is not afraid to ask for what they want and you have only a vague idea of what you want, it is like going into a gunfight with no bullets in your gun.

Set your sights high. When you ask for a higher price, you allow yourself room to move--trading for other items in the sale you might want during the presentation.

The essence of selling is to make your request loud and clear, so the customer hears it. Don't be afraid to do just that. Don't be embarrassed to ask for the business.

24. You don't have a playbook

Comedians who cannot overcome the "hecklers" in the audience do not last long on the circuit. To solve this problem, they write down every heckle they are presented with. They write down their response and practice it over and over again until it is perfected. They keep this "heckle book" as a prized possession. As a salesperson, you can do the same thing with objections. A good way to start is to use the Abraham Lincoln formula and apply it to each objection in your "playbook."

Abraham Lincoln had a reputation as a lawyer for hardly ever losing a case. His strategy was to unknowingly use the feel/felt/found formula to perfection. However, he probably never heard of it.

Lincoln would never argue or attack an opponent. In fact, Lincoln, at first, would argue his opponent's case telling all the reasons why his opponent was right. He'd appear to agree to all the things his opponent said.

As his opponent was stating his case before the jury, Lincoln would write down everything that was said. Then he would begin changing the minds of the jurors by saying, "We all feel these things are true, and my opponent has skillfully presented them in a way that anyone hearing them would have felt the same. However, there are a few other things that influence this case, and when I present them, you will find that the way to vote will be obvious."

Then he'd begin slowly with his own arguments. He was a master at diplomacy, at getting people to change their minds and feel good doing it.

Lincoln probably invented the "feel/felt/found formula even though he never heard of it. The feel/felt/found formula can become one of your most valuable tools. Try this response when you get a negative reaction to the price you are presenting or the program you are trying to push through.

"I can certainly understand why you feel the price seems a little high."

"I don't blame you for wanting to get the best value for your money and at the same time keeping your cost down to a minimum."

"Every person I talk to has felt the same as you do when they first looked at the program."

However, after they found out that the small difference in

price for the higher quality product was actually the best investment they ever made they saw it from a completely different view."

"Why should I pay you all this money?" This is how I would answer using F/F/F...

"At first glance you are right, it may seem like a large investment. I have served hundreds of clients over the years Bill, and when I first presented my program, they also showed a slight concern, just as you are now. Once they realized the amount of value they were receiving in relation to what they were investing, it all made sense. Would you like to review the benefits both to you and your company? For example, how much bottom line profit would a 20% sales increase amount to in actual dollars? Etc."

The key to successfully using this tactic is to try and NOT use the words feel/felt/found, only the structure. It will come off sounding a whole lot more sincere.

25. You don't add value

A sales rep told me how he would go into an account with both a high priced and a low priced product. He would say that he was reluctant to show the higher priced product and said you probably don't want this high-quality product. Even though it is the best you can buy, the price is high – much higher than this cheap economy brand. He said that whenever he used this technique, the customer seemed to want what the salesperson was reluctant to sell.

Another sales rep recently told me a great story about how to keep from giving a discount or from having to negotiate the price. He was having a brake job done on his car, and the cost was $140. When he asked, "is that the best you can do" here is how he responded: "If you want to negotiate the price – the brake job will cost you $150!"

Think about what a great answer that is. What is he really saying? He is saying that I am already giving you the best price I can. He is saying that if you want to negotiate, I will raise the price to $150 and we can see if you can get me down to the bottom price of $140.

Reluctance is an important tool that can be used in selling. How? If you give a discount too easily or too quickly you have actually cheated the customer out of the feeling that he or she made a good purchase. Have you ever had the feeling that you paid too much for something? Where did that feeling come from? It came from the fact that the salesperson lowered the price too quickly. "Maybe I should have asked for a bigger discount?" You are thinking. "Maybe the salesperson has been overcharging me right along?"

A little thought and reluctance actually add value to the product or service.

I was sitting on the plane and the woman sitting next to me was in advertising sales. When I asked her what the biggest mistake was that she ever made in sales, here is what she told me. "I was calling on a pawn shop with my sales manager. He told me the bottom-line price was $1,500 but to try and get $2,000. He said to go down slowly and reluctantly so you "add value" to the program. When the customer asked for the price, I made a huge mistake said $1,500! The customer ended up paying $1,400, and I ended up getting chewed out!"

Here is another reason we shou d be slightly reluctant when giving a price reduction. An accountant once told me that I should forget the term "gross profit" and replace it with "contribution to overhead." He said that every time I lower the price I am giving part of the company away! The warehouse cost is .04%, the sales department cost is .04%, the transportation department is another .04%, administration cost is .04%, and the bottom line should be at least .04%. When you cut your price below .20% think about what part of the company you are cutting out and giving away!

You do not want to appear too hungry for the sale or too eager to give everything away. When you do a customer will be suspicious and begin to wonder why you are so anxious to make a sale.

If you give a discount too easily or too quickly you have actually cheated the customer out of the feeling that he or she made a good purchase.

26. You don't ask for the order

If everything has been done correctly up to the time to close, the close will come naturally. Let's assume we lack just that final touch that puts us in the class of a professional closer. What is that touch? First, the difference between an amateur and a professional closer are that both have the technique at hand; but the amateur uses it so crudely the buyer sees it and resents it. The professional by practice has polished his or her close to the point where it is relaxed and natural. Only one in four (25%) salespeople ask for an order after a sales presentation.

Make every call with a specific objective and close on that objective. The amateur, the beginner, still suffers from the delusion that he or she has accomplished something when he just "drops in" for a friendly call. The amateur excuses their lack of closing skill by saying to him or herself, "This will help me get in solid with the buyer." The amateur claims that the call has a lot of advertising value even though they made the call without a specific objective. They do not know that 20% of the salespeople on the force take 80% of the orders because they know how to close; that only one in four has a specific call objective and closes on that objective. To permit the buyer to defer the close is to leave the sale OPEN to a competitor. The Cutting-Edge professional KNOWS that it never pays to leave business on the table. You know that to permit the buyer to defer the close is to leave the sale OPEN to a competitor to walk in and take the harvest when you have planted and worked the crop. The salesperson who has polished the technique of closing to professional brilliance knows the fundamental difference between so-called "high pressure" selling and "low pressure". You know the value of intelligent, dramatic, forceful, suggestive closing when you feel in your heart you are rendering a great service by helping the buyer to decide something for the buyer's own good.

You are in the strong position because you have the advantage of working with an organized plan and objective.   After all, every sale is a contest, starting with two strikes on the buyer, because you have the advantage of working with an organized plan and an objective toward which you are steering him or her. The buyer is in the weak position of a follower on the defensive. The Cutting-edge professional has learned by sad experience that failure to close, to permit the decision to be deferred lets the prospect get cold when they might have been sold by the application of a quiet, smooth-running closing technique.

The direct close. The direct close is one of the best ways to close because you get it over with up front and there is no doubt about what you are there for. We literally start the presentation with the close. One thing that is extremely important in using this tactic is you have to know exactly what you want before making the call. An example: "I would like to have your ham business, what do I need to do to get it?". "I would like to have your produce business, what would my company and I have to do to get it?"

Choice close. The choice close is the most common close. However, it is often incorrectly used. If you wait until the end of the presentation and then try and squeeze the customer into a corner, they will resent it. The correct way to use this tactic is to build it into your presentation by offering two or three different choices, explaining all the differences as well as the features and benefits of each product, and let them choose the one that best fits their needs. For example, you could bring three different hams to a customer; a buffet ham, a PIT ham, and a football ham. As you were making the presentation, you would point out the advantages and disadvantages of each product, letting them make the final decision. The theory behind this close is that you give them a choice between something and something else and let them make a choice. You never want to give them a choice between something and nothing. This close is especially good for the "price buyer." You can show the low-quality product, the middle-quality product, and the high-quality product, pointing out that the higher price is really going to cost less in the long run.

The choice set up. Nearly everyone in sales knows how to use the choice close; what day would you like delivery, Tuesday or Wednesday? What pack size would be best for you, 12 or 24? You ask the customer to choose between something you want and something else you want and let them make the choice – you win both ways. Now let's take it to a higher level by including the element of contrast. Give them a choice between something they don't want and something they didn't know they wanted until you presented the choice.

Let's say you are going to sell a house to a prospective buyer. The price you want is $100,000. You first take them to a $125,000 house that is overpriced by $25,000. Next, you take them to a $75,000 house in need of $50,000 worth of repairs located in a poor area. NOW you take them to your perfectly priced house - $100,000. The choice for the buyer is clear.

How about the used car salesperson? They first show you an old clunker that is overpriced and barely runs. Next, they show you the car they really want to sell you. In your mind, you are comparing the differences and thinking about what a great bargain it is!

You are talking to a computer salesperson about purchasing a new system for your office. You tell the salesperson all your requirements who is adding everything up on your list. The salesperson now hits you with a whopping $10,000. As soon as you are over your shock, you are presented with another choice – a package deal for only $3,000. What a deal! What an easy choice to make. Of course, that is what they wanted to sell you in the first place.

Let's say you are going on a job interview and you are going to use the choice close set up. Arrange for two interviews, one immediately following the other. Have a friend go on the first appointment and have them intentionally screw up the interview. Then you go in, well prepared, on the second appointment for your interview and the choice becomes obvious.

If you think this sounds a little shady, consider this choice close set up used by undertakers. The Undertaker will first show you a low budget, low price casket that is carefully positioned in a dark corner of the showroom. Then they show you the higher priced casket and point out all the benefits. Compared to the low-end casket it is an easy choice to make.

What does this have to do with you?

The next time you present a product to a customer take two products instead of one. Take in an overpriced high-end product along with the one you want to sell. Show them the overpriced, high-end product first. After they get over their shock, bring out the one you wanted to sell in the first place, and it will seem like an easy choice.

Guarantee close. Before using the guarantee close, you have to be sure your company or the manufacturer will go along with it. It is similar to a closing tactic called the "puppy dog close." The pet store owner tells the parents of the little boy to take the puppy home over the weekend, and if they are not happy with it, they can bring the dog back on Monday. Of course, you know what will happen during the weekend, and the dog will never come back. When using this close in a more professional setting, you might tell the buyer to try the new coffee machine for thirty days, and if they are not happy with it, we will pick it up and reinstall the old one. Some companies have even gone so far as to buy out the existing supply of a competitor's product if they agree to try the new product for 30 days.

Time advantage. The time advantage creates a sense of urgency during the presentation. "While supply lasts" implies that there are several other salespeople selling the same program and if you don't put your order in right now you might miss out. "Limited time only" implies that the price will soon go back to the book price. "Sale ends Friday" also creates the feeling of missing out on an opportunity. "One time offer" is designed to put pressure on to take advantage of the promotion now or miss out altogether. "Longer shelf life" is also a way of taking advantage of time if the shorter shelf life of a competitor is causing a loss due to waste. "New inventory is higher" implies that the market has gone up and we are holding our price down until we sell out of our current stock.

Trial close. The trial close is designed to lower pressure by using the word "IF." If you decided to buy which portion or pack size would be best? If you decided to buy how many could you sell in a week? If you put this in stock would it benefit your customers? If you stocked this line for one year how much money would it save you?

These trial questions should be part of your presentation. The purpose is to see how close you are to the actual order in a low-pressure way. Build test questions into the presentation and use them often. The key is to start them with the trial word "IF."

"Ask a question" close. The ask a question close is based on the fact that it is sometimes hard for a customer to say yes, however, it is much easier for them to say "No." The magic question to ask is this: "Is there any reason why we shouldn't go ahead with this?"

If your first attempt doesn't get the response you want - ask a second time. Wait a short period of time then ask again as if we were asking for the first time. The theory behind this close is the time it takes for a new idea or concept to take hold. It takes time for the mind to work and when we ask the first time, there is a natural defense mechanism at work. However, after just a few minutes the buyer's mind will start making mental associations and will have more information available to make the decision. Anybody can ask once and accept a negative response.

Doorknob close. The reason this is a "last resort close" is because we should try everything else first. After they refuse to buy, close your presentation, put everything in your briefcase and act as if you have stopped trying. In some cases, you can actually go to the door, stop, turn around as if you have left and returned as a friend instead of a salesperson. This is designed to lower their guard. Then ask the question: "Where did I go wrong?" At this point look at your watch and make a commitment to stay 15 minutes longer   You will be amazed at the difference in the person you are trying to sell.

Silent close. The silent close is the most difficult to use because it seems so unnatural. The hardest thing for a salesperson to do is to be quiet for 30 or 45 seconds. When there is silence, it almost seems like we are not doing our job. However, just the opposite is true. We have to give the buyer a chance to think things over, and he can't do it if we are talking away. Keep in mind that the biggest complaint buyers have about salespeople is that they talk too much   After the facts have been presented try and remember one thought: Whoever talks first loses.

27. You try too hard to close

When a customer has made up their mind that they are going to buy, they buy, they do the closing.

From time to time you should try to discover just how much you have accomplished in transporting the person in front of you to a state where he or she sees themselves using what you have to offer to their advantage. This can be done with "qualifiers" put in the form of questions such as, "where do you plan to put this, Mr. Brown?"

The psychology of the "close" has been so talked about by sales experts that it has frightened more salespeople than it has helped. When a person has made up their mind that they are going to make their imaginary picture a reality, then they do the closing, they buy, you don't sell them except to make it easy for them to sign an order.

You started to close the moment you decided to call for the appointment. You are closing all the way through the process.

As your presentation proceeds, it should include steps which apparently fit into the running story but which actually are used by you to anticipate objections. The time to answer most objections is before they are brought up, during the presentation.

If you don't build rapport

If you don't get them talking

If you don't gain their trust

If you don't make a great presentation

If you don't overcome their objections

If you don't make it easy for them to buy

If you don't fit your product into their future

If you don't follow up on your promises

If you don't ask for the order

YOU WILL NEVER CLOSE

Usually, people who have never had to go out and ACTUALLY MAKE A SALE think that selling is all about closing.

28. You don't follow up

Only 10% of sales people follow up to a buyer's complete satisfaction. Do I know what my customer expects after the sale? No matter how hard you worked or how much you have discounted your price when you sell a customer, he or she then feels that you still owe them something. The perception on the part of the customer is that you, the seller, have not only gotten new business but also his or her money. There were many other salespeople after the same account and the same business, but you were chosen as the recipient.

Therefore, psychologically, you now owe your customer a favor. Even though you had to bend over backwards to get the order. That is why follow up is so important to keeping the business.

We have been calling on a particular customer for months and have never gotten to first base. They are polite; however, they keep telling us to come back at a later date. All of a sudden, we make a small sale!

As soon as we leave the account, we check the stock status. Everything is checked, and you drop a card in the mail that your customer receives the next morning confirming the order, delivery date and approximate delivery time. After we check to be sure everything was delivered, we make a follow-up call to be sure everything was alright with the product. We get a few small reorders and continue the same follow up strategies. And then the orders get larger. Soon we are the primary supplier. Later we are having lunch with the customer, and he lets us in on the reason he switched: YOU FOLLOWED UP, AND YOUR COMPETITOR DID NOT!

29. You don't use the magic words

In a study done by the Small Business Administration, they asked business owners why they felt customers stopped buying. Nearly all said their prices were too high. But when the agency surveyed the customers of these people to find out the real reason they left, here is what they found:

2%   died

3%   moved away

9%   cited price

14%   dissatisfied with the product

68%   felt their business was not appreciated

Think of it! Over half left because no one said thank you!

The agency also determined that it cost 6 times more to attract a new customer than it does to keep an existing customer!

What is the easiest way for a competitor to take a customer away from you? Why do you lose accounts to your competitors?

Here are some reasons that sound good: Our service isn't up to par. Our prices are too high. We have too many out-of-stocks. My competitor is better known in my market.

I have a surprise for you. When you lose an account, it is mostly due to one reason. I would say that 95% of all the accounts you lose to a competitor are for this single reason! This single reason will enable you to take away more business from your competitor than you can handle.

It's easier than you think. Here's why. Your competitors are taking their customers for granted. I guarantee it! Let me say that again in capital letters...

YOUR COMPETITORS ARE TAKING THEIR CUSTOMERS FOR GRANTED.

And do you know what else? So are you - I know, I know - you don't want to hear that. It's true - you know it, and I know it.

132

Let's put it to the test. Do you feel appreciated?
Probably not. Would you like a little appreciation? If your
answer is yes - you are not alone. In a recent survey
6,600 people were asked two questions:

1. Do you receive as much praise, recognition, and
appreciation as you feel you deserve?

6,415 SAID NO

2. Would you perform your job better if you were given
more praise, recognition, and appreciation?

6,495 SAID YES

This, of course, doesn't apply to you-you are in sales - it
is up to you to GIVE appreciation not GET it. The point is
- most people feel unappreciated.

Here's more proof - a real-life example: I was helping a
small distributor look for a way to promote their business.
We thought about a trade show, however, due to the
small size of the company we felt that it would be too big
of an undertaking. After a lot of talking we finally came up
with a program we called a "customer appreciation
dinner."

We contacted 20 of his suppliers and asked them to participate by serving dinner to the customers and at the same giving them the opportunity to show samples of their products. All the suppliers agreed, and we put together a buffet line concept with the theme being that we want to show our customers that we appreciate their business.

We decided to use an RSVP format so we would know how many people would show up, and we could tell the suppliers how many people they could plan on feeding. We arranged to have the dinner at a Holiday Inn with a room large enough to hold 108 people at one time.

We sent out 525 invitations expecting to get about 200 RSVPs. The invitation said, "When was the last time someone took you to dinner to show you how much they appreciate your business?"

Not knowing the power of our theme, "Customer Appreciation Dinner," we had 525 RSVPs! We had to turn the tables FIVE TIMES during the evening. Every restaurant in the small southern town was closed with a sign on the door saying "Closed - we went out for dinner."

The normal procedure is to get an account, wine and dine them during the honeymoon period, and then put them on autopilot. You are guilty of it, aren't you? Admit it.

How can you take away business from a competitor? Here's the secret. Get a small order from your competitor's customer and then show that you REALLY appreciate their business. Too simple? - You WILL stand out and be noticed.

Sure, you gave the customer a discount - THEY should appreciate YOU! Your customer is the one who writes out those big checks every week - they are not thinking about how much they appreciate the small discount they got - they are wondering if YOU appreciate the amount of business THEY are giving YOU.

Your customers pay your mortgage, put your kids through school, make your car payments, pay for your retirement plan. Your top twenty customers - Do you thank them enough? Do you show them that you appreciate their business? More than likely the answer is no.

Give your customers the attention and appreciation they are hungry for. Give your prospects the attention and appreciation they are not getting from their current supplier, and you will take away the business.

Few things are more gratifying than gratitude, and very few salespeople express their gratitude as much as they should.

Appreciation can go a lot farther than just saying thank you. How many thank you notes did you send last year? Your competitors are not doing it. It's the little messages of gratitude that will make a big difference.

I was sitting in a buyer's office when a fax came in for him. He seemed a little upset, so I asked him if there was anything wrong. He said a salesman had just left with a large order and he just faxed a thank you note.

I thought that was pretty good for a salesperson to take the time to send a thank you fax. However, the buyer said he was going to cancel the order, but because of the thank, you note it became too difficult to call and cancel.

You never know what insurance your thank you notes, follow up phone calls and extra attention is providing. Here is more proof.

Headquarters wanted to know why a small pizza shop was performing way beyond everyone's expectations. They were number one in a large national chain – yet located in a small town with a lot of competition. When they investigated, they found that before closing they would go through their deliveries and call everyone to make sure their pizza was good!

CAN YOU IMAGINE THAT? A thank you call from a PIZZA SHOP?

I just bought a new house. After the closing I never heard a peep from the broker - nothing - zero! I even had to call his office and tell them to come and get their sign out of my yard!

No - Service is not the reason you lose business.

No - Price is not the reason you lose business.

No - Your competitor's image in the market is not the reason.

No - it's none of those things.

The reason you lose, on average TWENTY-FIVE PERCENT OF YOUR BUS NESS EVERY YEAR is because you didn't listen to your mother when she told you to say, "Thank You."

For more information visit...

www.BobOros.com

Bob Oros has been a full time speaker and author since 1992 with over 2,000 speaking engagements in all 50 states and several international locations. Prior to starting his speaking career, Bob served six years in the US Navy as a Communications Specialist and then worked his way from a street sales person to the position of National Sales Manager for a Fortune 200 company.

CSP Award: In 2005, Bob was awarded the designation of Certified Speaking Professional (CSP) by the National Speakers Association and the International Federation for Professional Speakers. Fewer than 10% of all speakers worldwide qualify for this award.

Professional Writer: Bob is the author of more than 60 books on sales. As a past member of the Professional Writers Alliance along with 35 years of sales experience,

Bob writes his books and training programs in a way that will have your team members leaning forward asking for more.

Edmond, Oklahoma

Bob@BobOros.com
www.BobOros.com